THE 1900s
DECADE IN PHOTOS
A DECADE OF DISCOVERY

Jim Corrigan

Enslow Publishers, Inc.
40 Industrial Road
Box 398
Berkeley Heights, NJ 07922
USA

http://www.enslow.com

Library of Congress Cataloging-in-Publication Data

Corrigan, Jim.
  The 1900s decade in photos : a decade of discovery / by Jim Corrigan.
    p. cm. — (Amazing decades in photos)
  Includes bibliographical references and index.
  Summary: "Middle school readers will find out about the important world, national, and cultural developments of the decade 1900-1909"—Provided by publisher.
  ISBN-13: 978-0-7660-3129-6
  ISBN-10: 0-7660-3129-2
  1. United States—History—1901-1909—Pictorial works—Juvenile literature. 2. History, Modern—20th century—Pictorial works—Juvenile literature. 3. Nineteen hundreds (Decade)—Pictorial works—Juvenile literature. I. Title. II. Title: Nineteen hundreds decade in photos.
  E711.C67 2009
  973.91'1—dc22

                                                          2008042900

Printed in the United States of America.

092009 Lake Book Manufacturing, Inc., Melrose Park, IL

10 9 8 7 6 5 4 3 2 1

To Our Readers: We have done our best to make sure all Internet Addresses in this book were active and appropriate when we went to press. However, the author and the publisher have no control over and assume no liability for the material available on those Internet sites or on other Web sites they may link to. Any comments or suggestions can be sent by email to comments@enslow.com or to the address on the back cover.

Every effort has been made to locate all copyright holders of material used in this book. If any errors or omissions have occurred, corrections will be made in future editions of this book.

♻ Enslow Publishers, Inc., is committed to printing our books on recycled paper. The paper in every book contains 10% to 30% post-consumer waste (PCW). The cover board on the outside of each book contains 100% PCW. Our goal is to do our part to help young people and the environment too!

Produced by OTTN Publishing, Stockton, N.J.

TABLE OF CONTENTS

A group of students walks to school; behind them, smoke billows from busy steel mills at Homestead, Pennsylvania, circa 1905. As the new century began, many things were changing in the United States. Industry was booming. The United States produced more steel than any country in the world.

WELCOME TO THE 1900S

When the twentieth century began, there were about 1.6 billion people living in the world. When it ended, the world's population was more than 6 billion people. Humans thrived during the twentieth century. They also suffered many setbacks, including two world wars.

The first decade of the new century was exciting. The Industrial Revolution had changed the world. It began in Britain many years earlier, when people started using machines to make things. They also began working together in factories. These new methods spread around the globe. Machines and factories were soon everywhere. They gave rise to new inventions. Gains in science and medicine followed. On average, people began living longer.

Americans were very good at the new style of working brought about by the Industrial Revolution. American factories were efficient. Factory owners found new and better ways to make products. Small companies grew into giants. In the past, most people had lived on farms or in small towns. That was changing, too. People moved to the cities and took factory jobs. They earned steady wages and bought new products.

This colored drawing shows workers in a textile mill. Mill work was hard and dangerous.

Theodore Roosevelt, who became president in 1901, was very popular with the American public.

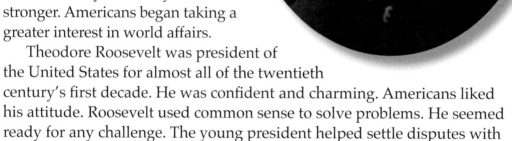

By 1900, the United States was starting to emerge as one of the world's powerful countries. At the time, countries in Europe controlled much of the globe. They had the largest armies. Their navies sailed across distant oceans. Suddenly, America joined them. The U.S. Army and Navy became stronger. Americans began taking a greater interest in world affairs.

Theodore Roosevelt was president of the United States for almost all of the twentieth century's first decade. He was confident and charming. Americans liked his attitude. Roosevelt used common sense to solve problems. He seemed ready for any challenge. The young president helped settle disputes with

(Opposite) An immigrant woman and her three children shell nuts at a table in their tenement apartment in New York. Often, families that were newly arrived in America found work they could do at home to supplement their income. According to social reformer Lewis Hine, who took this photograph, a family could earn an extra $4 a week picking nuts for a packing company. Other families found work making dolls or sewing for garment manufacturers.

HELP WANTED—FEMALE.

Miscellaneous Help Wanted—Female

UNSKILLED LABOR to be done at home. Apply 114 E. 16th, 6th floor.

other countries. He also cracked down on greedy factory owners. Theodore Roosevelt was a bold leader for a bold time in America.

Not all was perfect, however. Many factory jobs were unsafe and paid little. Many families were poor. Children had to quit school to work. They toiled long hours just to help their families buy food. Women were not considered equal to men. They did not have the right to vote. African Americans were often treated very poorly, especially in the South. They were denied the same rights as white citizens. It would take years for these inequalities to change.

These problems aside, the first decade of the twentieth century was a time of great excitement and anticipation. The world seemed to be getting smaller. People could send messages quickly over long distances, even across oceans. New machines were being created that would make it easier to travel to faraway places. For fun, people could watch stage plays and sporting events. But film was also getting started. Art, books, and music were also changing, as authors and artists began to explore new styles and ideas. The decade 1900–1909 was a time when people looked to the future.

The first machine-powered human flight occurred at 10:35 A.M. on December 17, 1903, at Kill Devil Hills, North Carolina. This famous photograph of that first flight shows Orville Wright at the controls of the airplane. His brother Wilbur has just let go of the right wing. This initial flight lasted only twelve seconds and covered 120 feet.

THE WRIGHTS TAKE FLIGHT

Orville Wright (1871–1948) was a good athlete as well as a talented mechanic.

As the new century began, people started to solve the mystery of flight. Since the dawn of time, people had watched birds fly. They dreamed of soaring through the sky, too.

Large balloons filled with hot air were a good start. However, they were slow and went where the wind blew them. People wanted a machine that could fly fast and in whichever direction the pilot chose. They got their wish in December 1903. Two brothers named Orville and Wilbur Wright invented the first airplane.

The Wrights were an unlikely pair for such a great advance. Neither one had finished high school. Still, they were good at building machines. As young men in Dayton, Ohio, the Wrights started a bicycle company.

Bicycles were fine, but Orville and Wilbur wanted to design other machines. Around the world, inventors were trying to create a flying machine. The Wrights eagerly read about these attempts. They

In May 1899, Wilbur Wright (1867–1912) wrote a letter to the Smithsonian Institution. In it, he asked for information that could be used to help build a powered flying machine.

were fascinated by the work of Otto Lilienthal. He was a famous German inventor. Lilienthal died in 1896, when one of his inventions crashed to the ground. The tragedy taught the Wrights to be careful. They used kites to experiment before trying to fly on their own.

By 1903, Orville and Wilbur were ready to test their machine. They called it the *Wright Flyer*. Its wings stretched 40 feet. The airplane weighed about 600 pounds by itself. But when the weight of the pilot was added in, the Wrights would have to get 750 pounds off the ground.

Before attempting a powered flight, Orville and Wilbur Wright spent several years making and flying gliders.

The Wright brothers' successful flights made them international celebrities. This French illustration shows Wilbur giving a public demonstration of the *Wright Flyer* in August 1908 at a horse racing track near the town of Le Mans, France.

WILBUR WRIGHT

The brothers needed a windy place for their attempt. They chose the coast of North Carolina. Because there was room aboard the *Wright Flyer* for just one pilot, the brothers flipped a coin to decide who would get to fly the airplane first. Wilbur chose heads and won. However, he would not be the first person in history to fly an airplane. The first attempt, on December 14, failed.

Three days later, the brothers tried again. This time it was Orville's turn. A cold breeze swept the dunes near Kitty Hawk, North Carolina. Carefully, Orville Wright nudged his fragile plane into the air. The first flight in human history lasted just twelve seconds. The plane barely reached a height of ten feet. It covered a distance of only forty yards. A passing seagull could have outpaced the *Wright Flyer* on that gray, winter day. It did not matter. As of December 17, 1903, birds no longer had sole reign of the sky.

WILBUR
WRIGHT
ORVILLE
WRIGHT

IN COMMEMORATION OF THE CONQUEST OF THE AIR

This monument commemorating the Wright brothers' accomplishments is located at Kill Devil Hills, North Carolina. The 60-foot granite tower was built in 1932.

PRESIDENT McKINLEY ASSASSINATED

William McKinley was born in Ohio in 1843. As a teen, he was a soldier in the Civil War. Later, McKinley studied law in New York. He worked as a lawyer in Ohio and then went into politics. He became president in 1897.

McKinley wanted to help American farmers and business owners. At first, he thought tariffs were a good way to do this. Tariffs are taxes on products made in other countries. They make foreign products costlier, so people will be more likely to buy products made in their own country. Soon after he was elected president, McKinley got the U.S. Congress to pass the highest tariff ever. But later, he changed his mind about tariffs. He felt that countries should instead try to trade goods fairly.

On September 6, 1901, President McKinley was in Buffalo, New York. He was greeting visitors to the World's Fair. People stood in a long line to shake the president's hand. A man named Leon Czolgosz waited in line for more than two hours. He was

William McKinley (1843–1901) was elected president of the United States as the Republican Party's candidate in 1896. McKinley won a large majority in the electoral college that year, with 271 electoral votes to 176 for Democratic Party candidate William Jennings Bryan. In 1900, McKinley was reelected by an even wider margin over Bryan, 292 electoral votes to 155.

holding a pistol wrapped in a handkerchief. When he got to the front of the line, Czolgosz pushed the gun against McKinley's chest and fired twice. The assassin was caught, but William McKinley died eight days later. Vice President Theodore Roosevelt became America's new leader.

On September 6, 1901, a man named Leon Czolgosz shot President McKinley in a public hall at the Pan-American Exposition in Buffalo, New York. Czolgosz was an anarchist—a person who wanted to do away with the government. At 4:07 P.M., he fired two shots from a .32 caliber revolver at the president. One bullet hit McKinley's ribs. The other passed through McKinley's stomach, colon, and kidney, lodging in his back.

Czolgosz was immediately tackled and arrested. The wounded president was quickly taken to a hospital. There, doctors removed one bullet. However, the doctors felt it would cause too much damage to try to find the second bullet, so they closed McKinley's wounds. At first, it appeared that McKinley would recover from the shooting. However, on September 12 his health took a turn for the worse. At 2:15 A.M. on September 14, William McKinley died from infection and gangrene caused by his wounds.

American Forces Go Abroad

For many years, the United States stayed out of world events. Americans cared little about what other countries did. By 1900, that was no longer true. U.S. troops were going overseas.

In 1898, America had fought and won a war against Spain. As part of the peace treaty, Spain gave control of some of its colonies to the United States. These colonies included the Philippine Islands, Cuba, and Puerto Rico. In the Philippines, many people thought the United States would grant them independence. When that did not occur, a war broke out in 1899. It took American troops three years of brutal fighting to defeat the Filipinos. More than 4,000 U.S. soldiers died in the war. So did 16,000 Filipino troops, along with many civilians.

Cuba gained its independence from the United States in 1902.

In 1902, American troops left Cuba. They had controlled the island since the Spanish-American War of 1898. Cuba officially became independent. But the United States still had a big say in how the country was run. The United States kept the right to send troops back into Cuba. American leaders wanted to control trade with the island. In 1906, U.S. troops went back to Cuba. They helped put down a rebellion that had broken out there.

American forces also helped put down an uprising in China. By the beginning of the twentieth century, China had lost a series of wars. Its government was weak. Foreign countries took advantage. They forced China to trade with them in ways

American soldiers defend a trench while fighting against Filipino rebels, 1901. After the Spanish-American War (1898), Spain ceded control over the Philippine Islands and Cuba to the United States. At the same time, though, many Filipinos wanted to establish their islands as a separate nation. They declared independence and set up a government, headed by Emilio Aguinaldo.

that did not benefit the Chinese. They also forced China to allow foreign citizens to live in the country. Many Chinese disliked this situation. In 1900, a group known as the Boxers started attacking foreigners. They wanted to rid China of all foreign influences. Troops from Great Britain, Germany, France, Japan, and several other countries sailed for China to stop the Boxers. President William McKinley sent 2,500 U.S. sailors and marines to join this effort. McKinley wanted the United States to get its share of trade with China. The Americans and their allies fought their way to the capital city of Beijing by August 1900. By September of the following year, the Boxer Rebellion had been crushed.

A unit of African-American soldiers stands at attention in Cuba, circa 1900. During the early twentieth century, African Americans were treated as second-class citizens in many parts of the United States. Despite this, many African Americans served with courage and distinction in the U.S. Army. African Americans overcame prejudice and racism to win battlefield honors in Cuba, the Philippines, and in other conflicts.

THE FIRST WORLD SERIES

Baseball became popular in the late 1800s. It was a smash hit in 1903, when the first World Series was played.

The new contest featured the best team from each league. The National League team was the Pittsburgh Pirates. The American League team was the Boston club. It did not have an official nickname but was often referred to as the Americans. (The team later became the Red Sox.)

Baseball fans went wild for the first World Series. Some went to see every game. They traveled by train between the two cities.

The Boston team had a great pitcher named Cy Young. Boston won five of the eight games played, becoming the first World Series champions.

Boston's star pitcher, Cy Young, had an outstanding season in 1903. He won twenty-eight games and lost only nine. Young pitched from 1890 to 1911, winning 511 games during his career. This is more than any other pitcher in baseball history.

A crowd of fans pours onto the field at Huntington Avenue Grounds in Boston after the first game of the 1903 World Series.

There was no World Series in 1904. A feud between team owners prevented it. Fans became very upset and complained. The owners quickly settled their dispute. The World Series resumed in 1905, and fans were delighted.

Pittsburgh's best player in 1903 was shortstop Honus Wagner, who had led the National League with a .351 batting average during the regular season.

Most people consider Honus Wagner one of the greatest shortstops of all time. He played from 1897 to 1917 and finished with 3,415 hits and a .327 career batting average.

RACING TAKES ROOT

Automobile racing began in Europe in 1894. It quickly caught on in the United States. Early races ran along country roads. In 1909, the famous Indianapolis Motor Speedway opened. Afterward, oval-track racing became the standard in America. The average speed of early races was only about 75 miles per hour. Today's race cars speed by at 240 miles per hour!

A poster from 1909 promotes auto racing at the Indianapolis Motor Speedway.

INDIANAPOLIS MOTOR SPEEDWAY
GREATEST RACE COURSE IN THE WORLD

TEDDY ROOSEVELT ENDS THE COAL STRIKE

At forty-two years old, Theodore Roosevelt became the youngest president in U.S. history. Americans liked his sense of fairness. Roosevelt cared about the rights of workers. He wanted business owners to treat their workers fairly.

In May 1902, coal miners in Pennsylvania went on strike. In a strike, workers refuse to do their jobs to protest something. The coal miners wanted better pay. They also demanded safer working conditions. The mine owners refused to meet their demands. As a result, 150,000 coal miners left their jobs. Months passed with no progress. Without coal, America faced an energy shortage during the winter.

Roosevelt used his power as president to break the standoff. He invited the mine owners to Washington, D.C. He also asked the leaders of the miners to come.

At the turn of the century, coal was the main source of fuel for heating homes, running factories, and operating trains and ships. In 1900, American miners produced more than 270 million tons of coal.

A group of miners prepares to exit a coal mine in Pennsylvania.

People wait in line to purchase coal in New York City, 1902. When coal miners went on strike, citizens worried about a coal shortage during the winter of 1902–1903.

Roosevelt told both sides to compromise. If they did not, he said he would order the U.S. Army to run the mines. The owners agreed to some of the miners' demands. In return, the miners ended their strike.

The mines were once again running. There was plenty of coal to heat homes and businesses during the winter. Theodore Roosevelt had solved the crisis. He also showed business owners and workers that they could resolve their differences.

Teddy Roosevelt Ends the Coal Strike

Early radio operators in New York copy down messages transmitted from ships at sea, circa 1910. New technologies such as radio and telephones helped speed up the pace of communication during the early twentieth century.

A French poster, printed to promote the 1904 World's Fair.

The ice cream cone was apparently invented at the World's Fair in St. Louis.

World's Fair. These included peanut butter, cotton candy, iced tea, and the waffle-style ice cream cone.

The fair brought money and prestige to its host city. At the time, St. Louis was the fourth-largest city in the United States. The fair closed in December 1904. By then, its profits had reached $25 million. Today, that amount would equal more than half a billion dollars.

The 1904 Olympic Games were held in St. Louis at the same time as the World's Fair. This third Olympic Games drew more than six hundred athletes from twelve countries.

FROM THE STAGE TO THE MOVIES

Before radio and television, many people went to the theater. They enjoyed a style of show called vaudeville. It had music, comedy, magic, and many other acts. In the early 1900s, some theaters added a new feature. It was the motion picture, or movie.

KLAW & ERLANGER'S ADVANCED VAUDEVILLE

TECK

NEW YEAR'S WEEK

MATINEE DAILY 2:30 P. M.

LAST OF THE BIG VAUDEVILLE BILLS

SPECIAL ATTRACTION

HARDEEN

The Handcuff King.

THE GEORGETTS | COLLINS & HART
The Two Strong Men. | BISSET AND SCOTT

ONLY VAUDEVILLE APPEARANCE OF

TRIXIE FRIGANZA

Late Co.–Star of "The Orchid".

MARGARITE AND HANLEY | JACK NORWORTH
The College Boy Monologuist. | NEW YEAR'S PICTURES

FIRST AMERICAN APPEARANCE

MAIDIE SCOTT

The Famous Irish Comedienne.

Early movies were very short. They ran only for about ten minutes. Most were comedies. People liked movies, but only as an amusement between live acts. Nobody imagined that movies could be exciting. A man named Edwin S. Porter changed everything in 1903. He made a serious film called *The Great Train Robbery*.

Vaudeville was one of the most popular forms of entertainment. Each evening's performance was usually made up of several unrelated acts.

This scene from *The Great Train Robbery* shows armed bandits forcing a telegraph operator to stop an approaching train. The 1903 silent film, which was produced by Thomas Edison's company, contributed greatly to the development of the modern movie industry.

Porter's new movie thrilled audiences. It was fast-paced and had gripping action scenes. *The Great Train Robbery* was only twelve minutes long. And, like all other movies of the time, it was in black and white and had no sound. However, it showed movie companies that people liked serious films. Because of Edwin S. Porter, movies became longer and more exciting. Eventually, sound and color would be added, too. Vaudeville remained popular through the first decade of the twentieth century and beyond. However, movies gradually started to replace it.

The plot of *The Great Train Robbery* was inspired by a real event—a train robbery committed by Butch Cassidy and his gang in Wyoming in August 1900.

This Japanese woodblock print depicts the surprise nighttime attack by Japanese cruisers on the Russian fleet at Port Arthur in February 1904. Japan's victory in the Russo-Japanese War established the island nation as an up-and-coming world power.

WAR ERUPTS BETWEEN JAPAN AND RUSSIA

Japan and Russia were rivals in Asia. Both nations built ships to control the Pacific Ocean. They also sent troops to occupy Korea. The two rivals became hostile toward each other. In 1904, Japan and Russia went to war. There was much at stake. The winner would become the leading power in East Asia.

Japanese soldiers watch as a train carrying relief supplies enters Manchuria.

Russian soldiers look down at a trench filled with the bodies of dead Japanese troops near Port Arthur, 1905.

For Japan, the war was a chance to test its new military strength. From the 1600s to the mid-1800s, Japanese leaders had kept their country isolated. During that time, the Industrial Revolution had transformed much of the world. But it was unknown in Japan. As a result, Japan had fallen far behind other nations. In the late 1800s, Japanese leaders decided their country needed to catch up. These leaders wanted to make Japan a modern country as quickly as possible. They imported Western technology. They brought in foreign experts. They built better schools. They also built a powerful army and navy. Japanese leaders were eager to prove that these efforts had worked.

Russia had long been a power in Europe. However, Russian leaders sought control over Asia as well. In 1898, Russia built a seaport at Port Arthur. A large fleet of Russian ships docked there. Port Arthur was in the Manchuria region of China. It was very close to Japan. Japanese leaders viewed the fleet as a threat. Russian ground troops also arrived in the area. Japan decided that war was necessary to halt the Russians.

This illustration from a French magazine shows wounded Russian soldiers after a battle in Manchuria.

Japanese Admiral Togo Heihachiro (1848–1934) proved to be a brilliant naval commander during the Russo-Japanese War. During the Battle of Tsushima Straits in May 1905, Togo's battleships destroyed most of the Russian navy. The Japanese victory at Tsushima forced Russia to ask for peace.

The fighting began on February 8, 1904. The Japanese navy attacked the fleet at Port Arthur. Some sailors died, but no ships were sunk. People around the world expected Russia to win the war. They thought that Japan's new army and navy would fight poorly. They were quickly surprised. Japanese troops fought hard and won many battles. In January 1905, they captured Port Arthur. Four months later, Japan's navy won a huge sea battle near the coast of Korea.

Afterward, both nations agreed to hold peace talks. Theodore Roosevelt, the U.S. president, offered to help. He invited Russian and Japanese representatives to come to America for the talks. The delegates met in Portsmouth, New Hampshire. They worked out a treaty. President Roosevelt was praised for his role in the peace talks. He received the 1906 Nobel Peace Prize.

As the war's loser, Russia had to withdraw its forces from East Asia. Japan received Korea as a prize. The victory was a boost to Japan's world status. It also gave the Japanese military more power at home. People in Russia were already unhappy with their government. The loss to Japan made them even more upset. They revolted, but the Russian government survived—for the time being.

U.S. President Theodore Roosevelt (center) meets with Russian and Japanese negotiators during the peace conference at Portsmouth, New Hampshire, in 1905. The Treaty of Portsmouth gave Japan control over Korea and southeast Manchuria.

EARTHQUAKE DESTROYS SAN FRANCISCO

*E*arly on the morning of April 18, 1906, a terrible earthquake struck California. The quake was centered near San Francisco, but tremors were felt hundreds of miles away. Even people in Oregon and Nevada felt the tremors.

In San Francisco, buildings tumbled to the ground. Many fires started. Firefighters had no water with which to stop the blazes. The quake had broken the city's water lines. The fires burned for three days. In the end, 80 percent of the city was destroyed. More than 3,000 people died in the earthquake and fires. A quarter of a million people were homeless. Little was left but rubble.

The 1906 San Francisco earthquake was one of the worst disasters in American history.

San Francisco would be rebuilt. However, many people did not wait for that to happen. They went south to Los Angeles. The arrival of San Franciscans helped Los Angeles become the most populous city in California. Even today, the 1906 San Francisco earthquake ranks as one of the worst natural disasters in U.S. history.

The April 19, 1906, issue of a San Francisco newspaper reported on the scope of the disaster.

A view of the destruction in San Francisco, taken shortly after the fires were extinguished. The structure atop the hill on the right is the Fairmont Hotel, which still stands in San Francisco today.

The Jungle Shocks Readers

During the first decade of the twentieth century, factories were often dirty and dangerous. There were no safety inspectors as there are today. Some factory owners cared only about earning a profit. They did not care if their workers were in danger. They also did not care if their products were unsafe. Certain writers wanted the public to know of these outrages. These writers were called muckrakers.

The most famous muckraker was Upton Sinclair. In 1906, he wrote a book called *The Jungle*. It was about the stockyards of Chicago. Stockyards are places where animals are slaughtered and turned into food products. *The Jungle* described very unhealthy conditions at the stockyards. Readers were shocked to learn that their food came from such filthy places. There was a public outcry.

During the early twentieth century, working conditions in meat-packing plants were poor. The facilities were not clean, and the equipment was not safe.

During his lifetime, Upton Sinclair (1878–1968) wrote more than ninety books. His 1943 novel *Dragon's Teeth* won the Pulitzer Prize. Some of his other books explored the conditions that workers faced in industries other than meat-packing, such as coal mining, oil drilling, and auto manufacturing.

Congress quickly passed laws to make food preparation more sanitary. Upton Sinclair had made a difference. However, he was still unhappy. Sinclair had written *The Jungle* to show people the plight of stockyard workers. Instead, people focused only on food safety. Sinclair said he had aimed at the public's heart but hit its stomach instead.

When *The Jungle* was published in 1906, it became an immediate best seller. The book's success caused the American public to become outraged about the dirty conditions in U.S. meat-packing plants. As a result, Congress passed the Pure Food and Drug Act and the Meat Inspection Act of 1906.

Young girls operate meat grinders in the Armour meat-packing plant in Chicago.

THE JUNGLE
BY
UPTON SINCLAIR

DOUBLEDAY, PAGE & C.°
NEW YORK

The Jungle **Shocks Readers**

THE PHONOGRAPH BRINGS MUSIC HOME

Thomas Edison was one of America's finest inventors. He was a clever and tireless worker. During his life, Edison created more than a thousand inventions. Among these were the first practical electric light and a motion-picture camera. Edison also invented a machine called the phonograph.

With the phonograph, people could listen to recorded music. There are many ways to do that today. The CD player and MP3 player are just two examples. But in Edison's time, it was impossible. To hear music, people had to go to a concert or other live performance.

Edison's phonograph was an early form of record player. The records it played were fragile and broke easily. People did not mind. For the first time, they could hear fine music at home. Edison was surprised that people used his invention for music. He thought it would be better used for office work.

Thomas Alva Edison (1847–1931) poses with his original phonograph.

German-American inventor Emile Berliner (1851–1929) poses with the phonograph machine that he invented in 1888. Berliner's phonograph differed from Edison's because it played sounds recorded on flat disks, rather than cylinders.

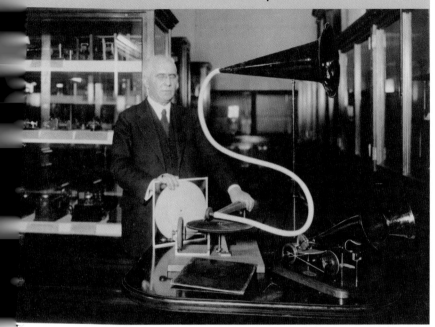

The hand crank on the side of this early phonograph was used to power the device. Turning the crank engaged a spring-wound motor, which would spin the record at the proper rate of speed.

By 1904, the world's best musicians were making records. Italian opera singer Enrico Caruso was among the first recording stars. By 1920, Caruso had made more than 260 recordings. The phonograph carried his voice into millions of homes. Edison's invention had changed music forever.

A magazine advertisement for a Victor recording by Italian opera singer Enrico Caruso (1873–1921). Caruso was the most famous singer of his time. He also was one of the first singers to make recordings of his performances.

The Phonograph Brings Music Home

A ship enters one of the locks in the Panama Canal. Since opening in 1914, the canal has been enormously successful. Each day, about forty ships pass through the forty-eight-mile-long canal, which connects the Atlantic and Pacific Oceans. The journey through the canal takes about nine hours.

Digging the Panama Canal

Sailors hated to travel between the Atlantic and Pacific oceans. To do so, they had to make a long and dangerous voyage around the tip of South America. As early as the 1500s, some people had dreamed of connecting the two oceans with a man-made waterway through Central America. A canal would save time, energy, and lives.

In the late 1800s, a French company tried to dig a canal through Panama. In some places, Panama is barely forty miles wide. But it is a rugged land of mountains and jungles. It also receives very heavy rains. The French plan was to create a waterway at sea level. Workers would have to cut through Panama's steep mountains. This proved impossible. Also, many workers became ill with tropical diseases, and about 20,000 died. Machinery rusted in the wet climate. After almost ten years of work, the French company gave up.

American leaders decided to try where the French had failed. In 1904, the United States began digging the Panama Canal. Everyone knew that the job would be extremely difficult. But the Americans had learned from French mistakes. First, they did their best to make sure workers stayed healthy. A U.S. Army

An American military doctor, William C. Gorgas (1854–1920), worked to eliminate two tropical diseases that had slowed progress on the Panama Canal, yellow fever and malaria.

A steam shovel excavates a section of the canal known as the Culebra Cut. Between 1904 and 1914, more than one hundred steam shovels were used to dig the canal.

doctor named William Gorgas studied the problem. He found that one of the deadliest tropical diseases—yellow fever—was spread by mosquito bites. That was also how malaria, another terrible disease, was spread. So Gorgas ordered chemicals to be sprayed on mosquito breeding areas, killing the insects. Gorgas also helped keep tens of thousands of workers from getting ill by making sure that they had plenty of clean water to drink.

American engineers avoided another mistake the French had made. Instead of trying to build the entire canal at sea level—which would require them to cut through mountains—the Americans decided to raise ships *over* the high ground. They did this by building a series of giant chambers called locks. Each lock has huge doors to separate it from the next one. A ship sails into the lock. More water is added to

General George W. Goethals (1858-1928) was appointed as chief engineer by President Roosevelt in 1907. Under Goethals's supervision, the canal was completed more than a year ahead of schedule.

The 1900s Decade in Photos: A Decade of Discovery

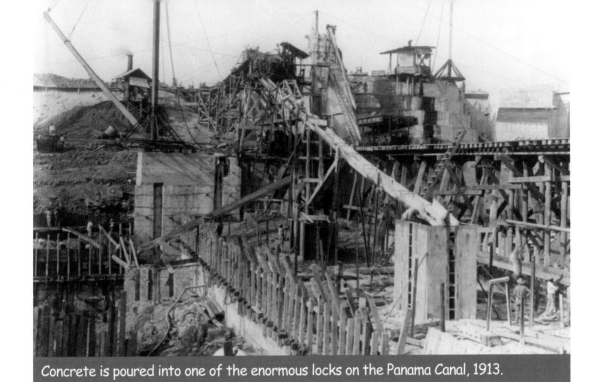
Concrete is poured into one of the enormous locks on the Panama Canal, 1913.

the lock, raising the ship higher. The huge doors are then opened, and the ship sails into the next lock. More water is added to that lock, raising the ship even higher. In this manner, a ship can climb steep terrain.

Building the Panama Canal was one of the greatest feats in human history. It took a decade to complete. There were many landslides and accidents. More than 5,000 workers died on the job. But the canal's opening made it possible for ships to travel between the Atlantic and the Pacific in less than ten hours, rather than five or six weeks.

For decades, the Panama Canal was run by the United States. In 1999, the United States turned over control to Panama. Today, more than 14,000 ships pass through the Panama Canal each year. Each ship saves thousands of miles on its journey.

A tugboat guides the first ship through the Panama Canal, February 7, 1914.

Oklahoma Joins the Union

In 1907, Oklahoma became the forty-sixth state. For some, this was a happy event. For American Indians, it was the end of a long and tragic story.

During the 1800s, America grew rapidly. As white settlers moved west, they took ancient tribal lands from American Indians. The U.S. government uprooted tribes from the southeastern part of the country and forced them to

During the 1830s, the U.S. government forced the Cherokee, Chickasaw, Choctaw, Creek, and Seminole tribes to give up their homes in the southern states. These American Indians were resettled in what became known as Indian Territory—present-day Oklahoma. This painting shows Cherokee Indians moving to new lands west of the Mississippi River during the late 1830s.

Prospective settlers rush into the Cherokee Strip, Oklahoma Territory, on September 16, 1893. Between 1889 and 1895, the U.S. government allowed settlers to claim 160 acres of land in certain parts of Indian Territory.

settle in present-day Oklahoma. The area was known as Indian Territory. Tens of thousands of Choctaw, Seminole, Cherokee, and others were moved there. The long journey from their homelands claimed many lives. American Indians remember it as the Trail of Tears.

By the 1880s, white settlers wanted land in the Indian Territory. Though it was against the law, whites began moving there. The tribes slowly disappeared. By 1907, only 9 percent of the people living in Indian Territory were American Indians. Congress granted them U.S. citizenship.

Indian Territory became a candidate for statehood. Some American Indians were against this. But others accepted the change. They helped write the laws that would govern the new state. Oklahoma joined the Union on November 16, 1907.

A U.S. quarter commemorating Oklahoma's admission as the forty-sixth state was issued in 2008. The coin's design includes the date of statehood, 1907, along with an image of the state bird, the Scissor-tailed flycatcher, in flight over a field of wild flowers.

Oklahoma Joins the Union

Henry Ford Mass-Produces the Model T

During the first years of the twentieth century, the automobile was still a new invention. Only rich people could afford one. A man named Henry Ford wanted to change that.

Henry Ford was forty years old when he started the Ford Motor Company. Ford's goal was to make a good car at a low price. In 1908, he unveiled the Model T. It was a simple but well-made vehicle. The Model T cost just $825 to buy. People did not have to be rich to own one.

Henry Ford (1863–1947) established the Ford Motor Company in 1903.

Finished Model T autos wait at the end of a production line at the Ford plant in Detroit, circa 1917. In 1909, the Ford factory produced 18,000 Model Ts. By 1918, more than half of all cars in America were Model Ts.

Between 1908 and 1927, Ford produced more than 15 million Model T autos. A few of them can still be seen on the road today. The Model T—nicknamed the "Tin Lizzie"—changed the world by making cars affordable.

Ford kept his factories running smoothly. He used a method called mass production. This method makes it possible to manufacture large quantities of a product at low cost. A key feature of mass production is the assembly line. On Ford's assembly line, each worker added a part as an unfinished car rolled past. By the time a Model T reached the end of the line, it was finished. At its peak, Ford's assembly line produced a new car every three minutes.

Henry Ford's methods were so efficient that the price of his car actually went down. By 1916, a new Model T cost just $360 to buy. Soon, half of all cars on American roads were Model Ts. Many other companies copied Ford's methods. Mass production is still widely used today.

PABLO PICASSO AND MODERN ART

The first decade of the twentieth century brought many big changes. Art was no exception. There were new styles and subjects. In the past, artists had focused on scenes from nature, history, or mythology. By 1900, paintings were more vivid. They expressed thought, feeling, and emotion. Modern art had arrived.

Pablo Picasso helped define modern art. Picasso dedicated his life to painting. Born in Spain in 1881, he was the son of an art teacher. By age twenty, Picasso had created his own style of painting. Using only shades of blue, he created touching scenes of poverty and sadness. In 1904, Picasso's Blue Period gave way to his Rose Period. He used red colors to portray circus performers and other entertainers.

Influential Spanish artist Pablo Picasso (1881–1973) stands in his studio. Picasso was one of the most important artists of the twentieth century.

Georges Braque (1882–1963) created this cubist painting, titled "Woman with a Mandolin," in 1910. Along with Picasso, Braque developed the new art movement during the early 1900s.

Later in the decade, Picasso started painting strange shapes. His work featured sharp angles and flat planes. He created images that were impossible in real life. The style came to be known as cubism. Picasso's new method was so radical that even some of his fellow artists disapproved. Regardless, Picasso's brilliance was eventually recognized. He inspired future generations of artists. Today, Picasso's paintings hang in the world's best museums.

Austrian artist Gustav Klimt (1862–1918) created his most famous work, "The Kiss," in 1907. Like the cubist paintings, "The Kiss" departs from nineteenth-century artistic traditions. However, "The Kiss" does represent its subjects more realistically than the abstract cubist paintings.

Pablo Picasso and Modern Art

This photograph, taken by the Hubble Space Telescope, shows hydrogen gas and dust in the Eagle nebula, some 7,000 light-years away from Earth. In the early 1900s, discoveries by physicists like Albert Einstein and Max Planck helped to improve human understanding of the universe and its properties. Their work made possible many scientific advances during the twentieth century.

BRILLIANT MINDS, GREAT DISCOVERIES

Albert Einstein was a physicist. He sought to understand the forces of nature and the universe. Sigmund Freud was a psychiatrist. He wished to know the mysteries of the human mind. Both men made amazing discoveries.

As a child, Albert Einstein had little interest in schoolwork. He thought his teachers were boring. Einstein preferred to teach himself. At age twelve, he learned geometry on his own. The study of lines, angles, and shapes fascinated him. It led him to a related field called physics. Physics is the science of matter and energy. Physicists explore natural properties like gravity and light.

German physicist Albert Einstein (1879–1955) is best known for his Theory of Relativity. This theory describes the relationship between matter, time, and space.

One of the earliest supporters of Einstein's theories was Max Planck (1858–1947). Planck was a highly respected scientist who had published papers on the nature of light and radiation. In 1901, Planck proposed a theory that became the basis for a new branch of physics, known as quantum physics. This theory describes the properties of the basic building blocks of the universe: the atom, as well as even smaller particles that make up atoms.

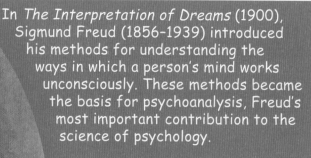

In *The Interpretation of Dreams* (1900), Sigmund Freud (1856–1939) introduced his methods for understanding the ways in which a person's mind works unconsciously. These methods became the basis for psychoanalysis, Freud's most important contribution to the science of psychology.

Young Einstein did more than just study. He also liked to play the violin. Still, his favorite activity was thinking about physics. After graduating from school, he took an office job. The work was dull but easy. It gave him plenty of free time. He used that time to think about how the universe works. Einstein never believed something just because it was written in a book. He always wanted proof. That trait helped him find answers to questions that other scientists had never even thought to ask.

In 1905, Einstein wrote three brilliant physics papers. They were about the nature of light and the motion of molecules. Molecules are tiny particles. Most of Einstein's peers could not grasp his amazing theories. Therefore, they chose to ignore the theories. It would take years for Albert Einstein to gain full acceptance.

Like Einstein, Sigmund Freud also disliked schoolwork. As a result, it took him three years longer than normal to graduate from medical school. Afterward, Freud studied diseases of the human body. However, his true passion was not the body, but the mind. Freud opened a psychiatry practice in his hometown of Vienna, Austria. He began working to prove a theory. Freud believed that traumatic, or extremely upsetting, events could affect a person's mental health. He found proof that the human mind sometimes buries painful memories. Freud sought to cure patients by uncovering their buried memories.

Most doctors initially rejected Freud's work. However, by 1906, he had gained a small group of followers. Sigmund Freud did not receive full recognition until well after his death in 1939. Some of his ideas were later abandoned. Regardless, Freud is still considered the father of modern psychiatry.

The first vacuum tube was invented in 1904 by John Ambrose Fleming (1849–1945), a British electrical engineer. The vacuum tube would become an important part of radios and other electronic equipment during the first decade of the 1900s. Vacuum tubes would later be used in televisions, radar systems, telephone networks, and early computers.

In 1907 a Belgian chemist named Leo Baekeland (1863–1944) developed the first man-made plastic, or synthetic resin. This hard substance, called Bakelite, could be molded into any shape. It would also maintain its shape after being heated. Bakelite was originally used to make parts for the electrical industry. Today, it is impossible to imagine a world without plastics.

REACHING THE NORTH POLE

The North Pole is located in the Arctic Ocean. It is so cold there that ice always covers the water. The North Pole is a very barren and unforgiving place. Before 1909, nobody had ever been there. That year, though, a team of explorers set out to reach the North Pole.

An American named Robert Peary led the team. Peary was a skilled explorer. He had been on Arctic journeys before. Peary's first two attempts to reach the

Robert E. Peary (1856–1920) spent much of his life exploring the Arctic. While mapping Greenland in the late 1880s and 1890s, Peary learned a lot from the Inuit (Eskimo) people about how to survive in the frigid climate. Unlike others who attempted Arctic expeditions, Peary dressed in furs and learned how to build igloos for shelter.

Matthew Henson (1866–1955) accompanied Robert Peary on many of his expeditions, including Peary's three attempts to reach the North Pole. Henson later wrote that on the final leg of the expedition, Peary had sent him ahead as a scout. As a result, Henson said that he had been the first person to cross the pole. He planted an American flag at the spot.

North Pole, in 1898–1902 and 1905–1906, failed. In July 1908, Peary set out with twenty-three men on a third expedition. Peary's team included an African American named Matthew Henson. Henson helped guide the group during its journey. There were also four Inuit guides. Inuit people are native to the Arctic region.

The team endured bitter cold. They traveled across frozen plains of shifting ice. Finding the North Pole was difficult. It was just another swath of snow and ice. However, on April 6, 1909, the explorers finally reached their goal. They were the first humans to set foot on the North Pole. Later, another explorer named Frederick Cook claimed to have reached the North Pole first. However, Cook had no proof, so his claims were rejected.

The cover of a French magazine from 1909 shows Robert Peary and Frederick Cook fighting over the North Pole. At first, many people believed Cook (1865-1940), who was a respected explorer in his own right. However, Cook could not produce proof that he had actually reached the North Pole.

Reaching the North Pole

THE NAACP IS FOUNDED

The Civil War ended slavery in the United States. However, it did not end racial bias (prejudice) and hatred. African Americans were still treated poorly. A small group of African Americans and whites chose to fight racism. In 1909, they formed the National Association for the Advancement of Colored People (NAACP).

Two important founders of the NAACP: Mary White Ovington (left) and W. E. B. Du Bois at a ceremony in Atlanta, circa 1920. Ovington (1865–1951), became the NAACP's first executive secretary. She remained deeply involved with the organization as an administrator and board member for the next thirty-eight years. Du Bois (1868–1963) was an influential African-American writer and political activist.

A year earlier, a vicious race riot had broken out in Springfield, Illinois. Several African-American citizens were killed. The riot proved that racism was still a big problem in America. More than forty concerned people met in New York City. The African-American scholar W. E. B. Du Bois was

Born into slavery during the American Civil War, Ida Wells Barnett (1862–1931) became an important advocate of civil rights for African Americans. She spoke out against racial segregation and the practice of lynching—illegal executions of African-American men by violent mobs. Wells Barnett took part in the meeting at which the NAACP was founded.

Throughout the NCAAP's history, the organization has worked to improve conditions for African Americans. Here, members of the NAACP hold signs demanding civil rights during the March on Washington, August 28, 1963.

their leader. They created the NAACP. Its goal was to promote fair treatment for all Americans.

Since its founding, the NAACP has worked to stop racism. It fought unfair laws designed to keep African Americans from voting. It also fought a policy called segregation. Under segregation, African Americans were kept apart from whites. They ate in separate restaurants, went to separate schools, and so forth. Segregation lasted in some Southern states until the 1960s. Today, the NAACP continues to promote equal rights for all.

The NAACP Is Founded

LOOKING AHEAD

The decade 1900–1909 was a time of discovery and progress around the world. Scientists like Albert Einstein and Wilhelm Roentgen advanced humanity's understanding of the universe. Inventors like Guglielmo Marconi and the Wright brothers laid the foundations for radio communication and air travel. Thomas Edison helped bring wondrous new gadgets, including the phonograph and the electric light, into people's homes. Henry Ford made the automobile affordable. People's lives had become more comfortable. Many people looked forward to the coming years with great anticipation. It seemed that life would just keep getting better and better.

This optimism would be shattered during the next decade. Mass-production methods would be used to churn out weapons rather than automobiles or other goods to make life better. Millions of people would die in the biggest war the world had ever known. Millions more would die in a worldwide disease epidemic that science proved powerless to halt.

In the United States, these tragedies would hit hard. But the country continued to expand during the decade 1910–1919. Two more states would be added to the Union. And America's importance on the world stage would continue to grow.

During the decade 1910–1919, the world's most powerful nations would become drawn into a devastating conflict. Approximately 20 million people were killed during the world war that took place from 1914 to 1918.

CHRONOLOGY

1900—The Boxer Rebellion erupts in China. Hawaii becomes a U.S. territory. American soldiers fight in the Philippines.

1901—In September, President William McKinley is shot and killed. China's Boxer Rebellion ends. Pablo Picasso begins his Blue Period.

1902—Cuba obtains independence from the United States. The Pennsylvania coal strike begins in May and ends in October.

1903—Boston defeats Pittsburgh in baseball's first World Series. On December 17, the Wrights make their first successful airplane flight.

1904—The Russo-Japanese War erupts in February. Construction of the Panama Canal begins. Picasso enters his Rose Period. The St. Louis World's Fair runs from April to December.

1905—Albert Einstein publishes three landmark physics papers. Japan wins its war with Russia.

1906—Upton Sinclair publishes *The Jungle*. On April 18, a huge earthquake rocks California and starts fires in San Francisco, destroying most of the city. Congress passes the Meat Inspection Act and the Pure Food and Drug Act.

1907—In November, Oklahoma becomes the forty-sixth state of the Union.

1908—Henry Ford unveils the Model T. President Theodore Roosevelt declines to seek another term in office. William Howard Taft wins the November election by a wide margin.

1909—Robert Peary's Arctic expedition reaches the North Pole in April. In May, equal rights advocates meet in New York City to form the NAACP.

GLOSSARY

assassin—A person who murders an important figure, such as an elected official.

civilian—A person who is not a member of the military.

delegate—An agent or representative to a conference.

Filipino—A person from the Philippine Islands.

mass production—A method of manufacturing large quantities of goods at a low cost through the use of assembly lines, machine tools, and other processes.

muckraker—A person who writes about hidden social problems.

physicist—A scientist who studies matter and energy.

psychiatrist—A medical doctor who treats mental or emotional illnesses and disorders.

radiation—Energy that travels in rays or waves, such as light or X-rays.

radical—Unusual and extreme.

sanitary—Clean and free of germs.

tariff—Fees placed on goods imported from other countries.

FURTHER READING

Bausum, Ann. *Muckrakers: How Ida Tarbell, Upton Sinclair, and Lincoln Steffens Helped Expose Scandal, Inspire Reform, and Invent Investigative Journalism.* Washington, D.C.: National Geographic Children's Books, 2007.

Bobek, Milan, editor. *Decades of the Twentieth Century: The 1900s.* Pittsburgh, Pa.: Eldorado Ink, 2005.

Cooke, Tim. *Disasters: 1906 San Francisco Earthquake.* Milwaukee, Wis.: Gareth Stevens Publishing, 2005.

Edge, Laura B. *William McKinley.* Minneapolis, Minn.: Twenty-First Century Books, 2007.

Elish, Dan. *Theodore Roosevelt.* New York: Marshall Cavendish Children's Books, 2007.

Hamen, Susan E. *The Wright Brothers.* Edina, Minn.: Abdo Publishing Co., 2007.

Mann, Elizabeth, and Fernando Rangel. *The Panama Canal: The Story of How a Jungle Was Conquered and the World Made Smaller.* New York: Mikaya Press, 2006.

Sonneborn, Liz. *Guglielmo Marconi: Inventor of Wireless Technology.* New York: Scholastic, 2005.

Yeatts, Tabatha. *Albert Einstein: The Miracle Mind.* New York: Sterling Publishing, 2007.

INTERNET RESOURCES

<http://kclibrary.lonestar.edu/decade00.html>
"American Cultural History, 1900–1909" is an online resource from the Lonestar College-Kingwood Library. It contains sections on art and architecture, books and literature, education, fads and fashion, and much more.

<http://www.aip.org/history/einstein/>
A detailed exploration of Albert Einstein's life and work, including his great discoveries of 1905, presented by the American Institute of Physics.

<http://www.sportingnews.com/archives/worldseries/1903.html>
Journalists from the Sporting News provide a vivid description of baseball's very first World Series in 1903.

INDEX

Index

PHOTO CREDITS